DANNY BRINKLEY

LET'S GET IT TOGETHER

Let's Get It Together by Danny Brinkley

This book is written to provide information and motivation to readers. Its purpose is not to render any type of psychological, legal, or professional advice of any kind. The content is the sole opinion and expression of the author, and not necessarily that of the publisher.

Printed in the United States of America.
ISBN   978-1-955363-90-7 (pc)
ISBN 978-1-955363-91-4 (e)

Lettra Press books may be ordered through booksellers or by contacting:
Lettra Press LLC
30 N Gould St. Suite 4753
Sheridan, WY 828011
1 307-200-3414 | info@lettrapress.com
www.lettrapress.com

Chris awoke to the warm sunshine streaming through the window and the smell of his favorite breakfast of buttery bagels toasting in the kitchen. The weather man on the radio alarm clock was giving his usual weather report for the coming day. "It's a beautiful sunny morning but this afternoon, there's going to be clouds with a high chance of showers."

Excited for what the day was going to bring, Chris jumped out of bed to pick out the clothes he would wear for the day.

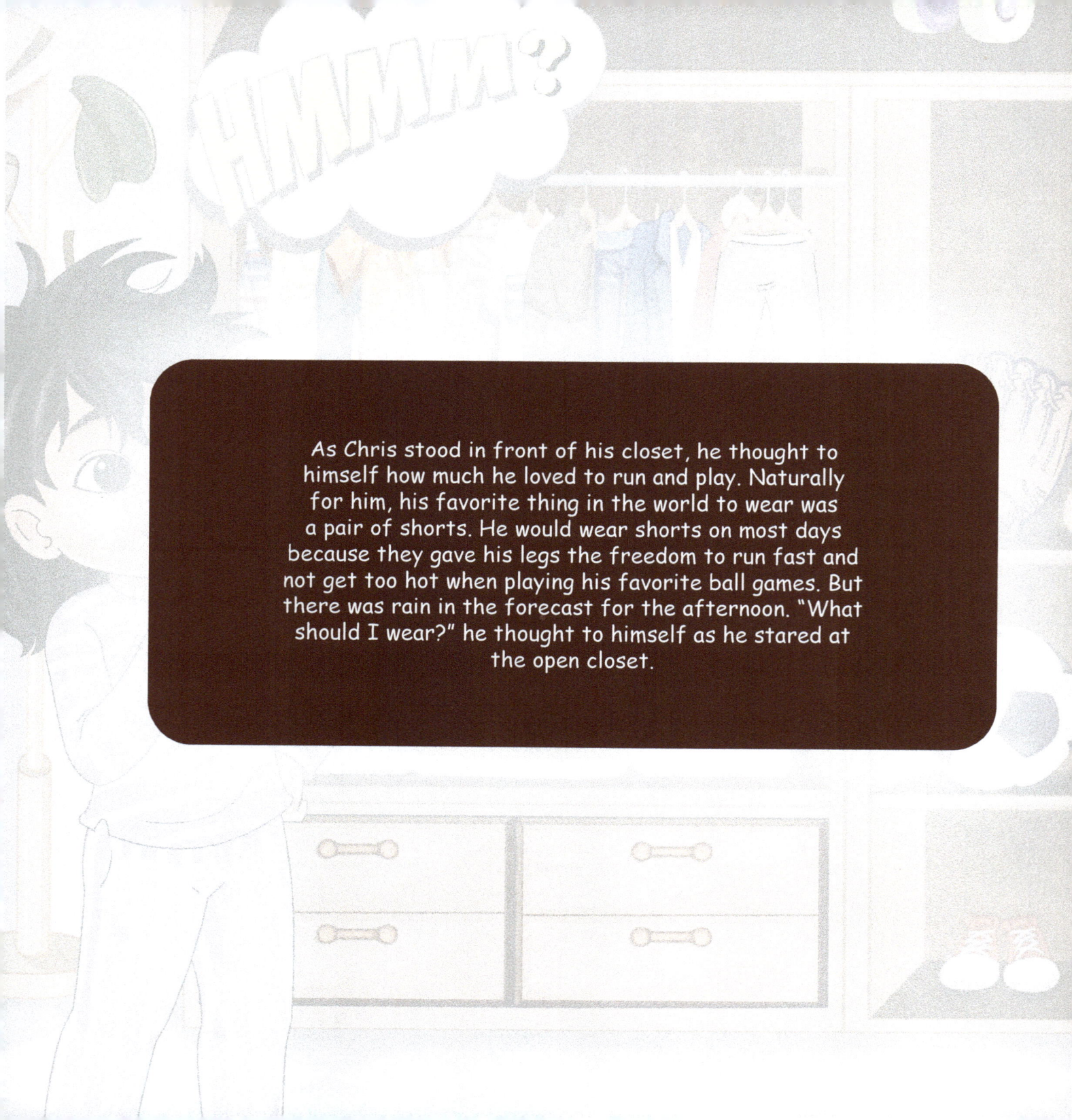

As Chris stood in front of his closet, he thought to himself how much he loved to run and play. Naturally for him, his favorite thing in the world to wear was a pair of shorts. He would wear shorts on most days because they gave his legs the freedom to run fast and not get too hot when playing his favorite ball games. But there was rain in the forecast for the afternoon. "What should I wear?" he thought to himself as he stared at the open closet.

He remembered that the weather in the afternoon was going to be rainy so shorts might not keep him warm. But if he wore pants, it might make him too hot when he played.

"What to wear?" he thought to himself again.

All of a sudden, Chris remembered those special pants that he got for his birthday, the ones that had zippers on each leg so they turned from pants into shorts. After putting them on, he looked in the mirror and noticed how sometimes, combinations of things could be good— some things were better when you put them together.

After getting dressed, Chris heard one of his favorite sounds in the whole world, his mother's happy voice calling him for breakfast.

"Chris, breakfast is ready!" The smell of the toasted bagel was so enticing he could almost taste it. Chris rushed out to the kitchen to get to his favorite spot at the table before his sister could.

"Phew!" Chris made it just in time while his sister was still brushing her long hair. "Thank goodness," Chris thought to himself.

His sister came out and looked a little disappointed that Chris got there first, but sat down anyway as their mother set down breakfast.

She was such an awesome mom that she made each of them their own favorites for breakfast. For Chris, there was nothing quite so delicious as a perfectly toasted bagel with delicious butter or cream cheese. His sister Anna's favorite breakfast was always a simple fried egg with salt and pepper.

Like most mornings, there was the usual discussion as to whose breakfast was better.

Sometimes it was nutrition-based, other times it was simply a matter of opinion on which one tasted better.

"Bagels are carbohydrates so they give you good energy so you can run fast and play for a long time without getting tired," said Chris.

"Well..." said Anna, "eggs have cholesterol that helps your brain work hard in school so you can get good grades."

Just then, their mother chimed and said, "I have an idea."

She then took one of the fried eggs and placed it between the two halves of a toasted bagel. She cut it down the middle and gave each of them a half.

"Here, try this," their mother said softly. The combination was delicious! "And you can have great energy from the carbohydrates, and good brain power from the cholesterol in the eggs. Not to mention, it tastes delicious!" their mother continued.

After the both of them tasted it, there was silence at the table, other than the smacking of their lips. They were enjoying the new combination of eggs and bagels together in a breakfast sandwich so much.

After finishing their breakfast, they heard the beep beep of the bus pulling up outside.

"Time to go," their mother said while grabbing their lunches.

They each raced over to the coat rack, by the door, grabbed their jackets and put them on, gave their mother a kiss on the cheek, said goodbye, and hurried out the door.

As the final morning recess bell rang throughout the hallways of the school, all of the children scrambled to take their seats.

"All right children," the teacher, Miss Joy, exclaimed, doing her best to calm the excited and chatty little kids. "This morning we are going to talk about colors. We are going to talk about all the different colors and combinations of colors. Let's start off by naming each of our favorites."

Miss Joy then went around and asked each student to name their favorite color, and what they liked about it. She first called on a young girl in the front named Isabella, who was waving her arms frantically.

Isabella said, "My favorite color is Yellow. It reminds me of my mother's yellow work dress, the one she is always wearing when she comes home from work." She always felt a little safer when her mom got home. "Yellow really makes me feel comfortable and reminds me of safety."

"That's great!" exclaimed Miss Joy. "Yellow is often used in safety situations such as caution signs and areas to be aware of."

Next, Miss Joy called upon a student sitting just behind Chris named Trevon.

"My favorite color is Red because it is very bright and reminds me of my red shoes which help me run really fast."

"That's great again, Trevon," said Miss Joy. "Red is often thought of as a powerful color so maybe that power of red is helping you run fast."

As Miss Joy went through many of the other students and the rainbow of their favorite colors, it seemed to Chris that she might miss him, so he began frantically waving his hands backand-forth in hopes that she would call on him next.

Of course, Miss Joy would never forget Chris and she called on him next. Chris loudly and proudly exclaimed, "My favorite color is Blue. I think it is the best color because it is the color of the ocean, the sky, and the planet when you see it from space."

"That's true, Chris," said Miss Joy. "Blue is the color of our planet and many peoples' favorite color."

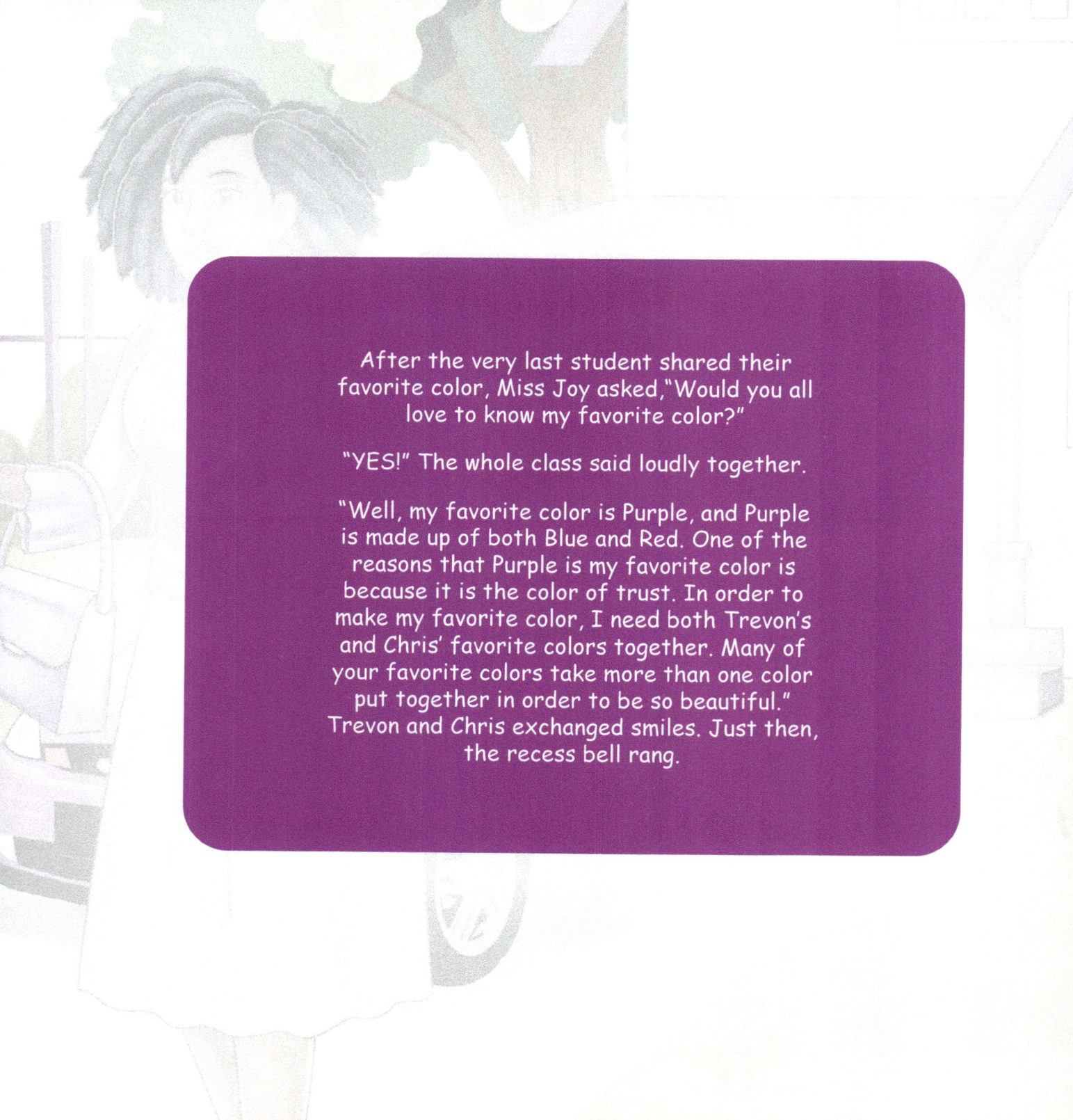

After the very last student shared their favorite color, Miss Joy asked, "Would you all love to know my favorite color?"

"YES!" The whole class said loudly together.

"Well, my favorite color is Purple, and Purple is made up of both Blue and Red. One of the reasons that Purple is my favorite color is because it is the color of trust. In order to make my favorite color, I need both Trevon's and Chris' favorite colors together. Many of your favorite colors take more than one color put together in order to be so beautiful." Trevon and Chris exchanged smiles. Just then, the recess bell rang.

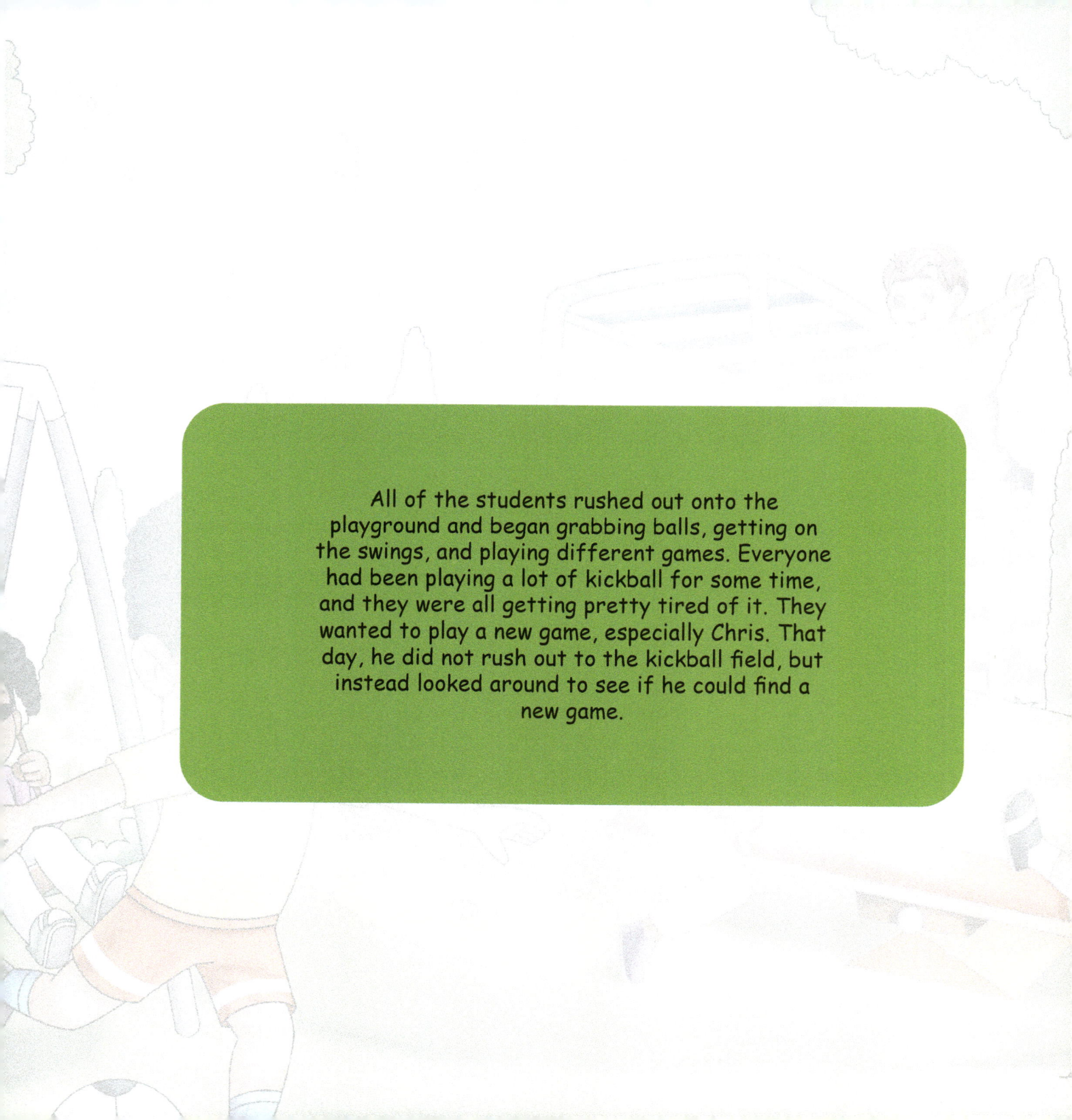

All of the students rushed out onto the playground and began grabbing balls, getting on the swings, and playing different games. Everyone had been playing a lot of kickball for some time, and they were all getting pretty tired of it. They wanted to play a new game, especially Chris. That day, he did not rush out to the kickball field, but instead looked around to see if he could find a new game.

He noticed one of the new kids hitting a red ball against the wall. The kid was by himself on the other side of the playground. Chris had wanted to meet the new kid for quite some time because he had seen him ride the same bus as him. It looked as though the new kid was playing one of Chris' favorite games that he had learned at his previous school. The game was called handball.

Chris approached the new kid and asked, "Are you playing handball? Because if you are, it is one of my favorite games. Are you familiar? If not, I can teach you. It takes both of us. My name is Chris."

The boy then said, "My name is Jason. I didn't think anybody would ever come talk to me. And I especially didn't think that anybody would know how to play handball at this school. Would you like to play with me?"

Chris said, "Of course. You can't play handball by yourself. It's definitely better together."

It didn't take long for many of the other students who were also looking for another game to be curious and ask about the game. Chris and Jason spent the rest of the recess explaining how to play handball and demonstrating for the crowd of children. Chris then started to notice just how awesome things really can be when you put them together, like new friends and new games.

The next class after recess was History, and today, the children were all going to present their projects on their own family history and heritage. Each child was to ask their parents to tell them the story of how their family originally came to this country.

Chris could not wait to present his project because he himself was an immigrant from another country called the Philippines. He was excited to share all the amazing facts about his country, like how it is made up of thousands of little islands that all together make up one awesome country. In this country, not only do you have some of the most delicious food in the world like mangoes, coconuts, and lumpia, but so many amazing nurses come to America and help keep people healthy. But of course, Chris would have to wait his turn.

After listening to a couple of stories from other students, Chris started to notice that many of the students also had parents, grandparents, and great-grandparents that came from different countries. In fact, every single one of the students in the class had a great origin story of where their family originated from.

Isabella had a great story of how her grandmother had to take a very dangerous journey, walking very many miles through the desert to come to this country. Altogether, the Mexican culture is very hard-working she worked very hard cleaning offices and homes so that Isabella and her mother would have a better life in this country.

Trevon told the story of how his family came from a beautiful place called the Congo in Africa, with many of the beautiful animals that everyone was familiar with, like gorillas, lions, and giraffes. Unfortunately, they had to leave their beautiful country as there was a dangerous mining operation for cobalt, which was to be used in batteries. People were being forced to work in dangerous conditions, so they came to America for a safer life. Trevon's father now owned a very famous and delicious African food restaurant in town and was very glad to live here.

Isha's father came from India before she was born because he always wanted to be a doctor. Now he was the town's pediatrician and was a doctor to many of the classmates, including Chris.

Kim's great great great grandfather came here from China to look for gold in California during the famous gold rush. Jason's great-grandparents came from a snowy country called Poland to practice their religion freely, because all religions were welcome in this country.

Every one of his fellow classmates' families came here because they wanted to have a better life, and all of those different people coming together is what really made this country great!

Chris attended the rest of his classes for that day and in no time at all, the bell for the ending of school rang. All of the students quickly closed their desks, turned off their computers, rushed to grab their backpacks, and hurried for the door.

Some students had their parents waiting for them outside to give them a ride home. Other students were able to ride their bikes, skateboards, or walk, but because Chris lived so far away from school and his mother was working, he had to take the bus.

Because he lived so far from school, he was one of the first students to be picked up in the morning, and one of the last to get off. The bus rides always seemed very long after school. Chris took his usual seat in the back of the bus and was ready for the long journey home.

He watched as each child got off of the bus and slowly but surely as usual, most of the students got dropped off before Chris.

Just then, Chris noticed that Jason was still riding the bus today and he remembered how much fun they had together showing everybody the new game of handball.

"Hey Jason!" Chris shouted. "Remember how awesome it was playing handball together today and showing everybody? It was like we were kind of famous on the playground. Would you like to come sit with me? I always get bored on these long bus rides."

"Of course," said Jason. "There are so many things that are better when you do them with someone else."

Chris and Jason spent the rest of the bus ride naming as many things as they could think of that were better together, and together they formed a new friendship.

Jason's stop came up and Chris couldn't help but feel a little bit sad because his new friend had to go home. As he looked out of the bus window to wave goodbye to his new friend, he noticed that there were small specks of water on the window. He saw Jason putting on his jacket and zipping on a detachable hood, just like Chris' pants. He realized that it had started to rain, just as the weatherman predicted this morning.

For a moment, Chris started to panic. He realized that he was wearing the special zipper pants-shorts. Reaching into his backpack, he pulled out the detachable pant legs and then zipped them on to his shorts.

Just as he was reminded by the rain to put on his pant legs, putting on those pant legs reminded him of all of the amazing things that happened to him just by doing them together.

Oftentimes, but not always, things go better when they are included together.

Different ideas and different ways of thinking come up, like a clothing solution such as his pants. They are great for those days that are sometimes both nice and stormy.

Two people can combine their favorite breakfast foods together to come up with an even better breakfast creation, even if they don't get along all the time (wink, wink!).

Just a few basic colors can be combined to make up all of the amazing hues of people, animals, plants, and really all of the beautiful things that we get to see every day that make this world so awesome to live in.

New people from different places, even different countries, come together to make new friendships and share their ideas, just like Chris and Jason sharing the game of handball and forming a friendship.

As Chris saw his stop approaching, he saw his family standing, all together, waiting for him at the bus stop. He couldn't help but smile and think of all the amazing possibilities that can come just by putting things together. He couldn't wait for tomorrow.

The end.